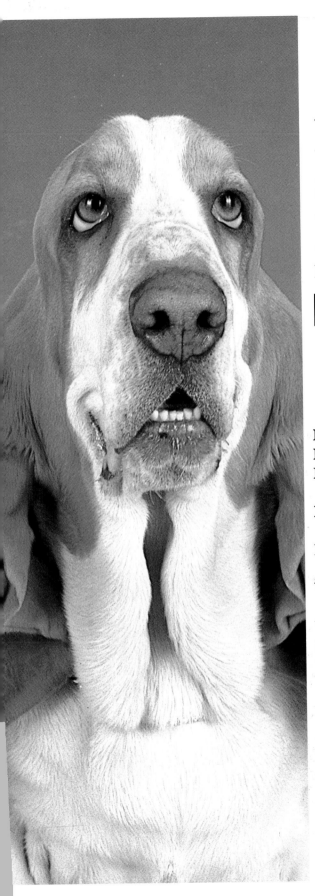

Puppies as a hobby

Dr. Herbert Richards

SAVE-OUR-PLANET SERIES

Contents

T.F.H. Publications, Inc.
1 T.F.H. Plaza•Third & Union
Aves.•Neptune, NJ 07753

A Brittany mom takes a breather while her pups check out an object of interest. Photo by Isabelle Francais.

Distributed in the UNITED STATES to the Pet Trade by T.F.H. Publications, Inc., One T.F.H. Plaza, Neptune City, NJ 07753; distributed in the UNITED STATES to the Bookstore and Library Trade by National Book Network, Inc. 4720 Boston Way, Lanham MD 20706; in CANADA to the Pet Trade by H & L Pet Supplies Inc., 27 Kingston Crescent, Kitchener, Ontario N2B 2T6; Rolf C. Hagen Ltd., 3225 Sartelon Street, Montreal 382 Quebec; in CANADA to the Book Trade by Macmillan of Canada (A Division of Canada Publishing Corporation), 164 Commander Boulevard, Agincourt, Ontario M1S 3C7; in ENGLAND by T.F.H. Publications, PO Box 15, Waterlooville PO7 6BQ; in AUSTRALIA AND THE SOUTH PACIFIC by T.F.H. (Australia), Pty. Ltd., Box 149, Brookvale 2100 N.S.W., Australia; in NEW ZEALAND by Brooklands Aquarium Ltd., 5 McGiven Drive, New Plymouth, RD1 New Zealand; in the PHILIPPINES by Bio-Research, 5 Lippay Street, San Lorenzo Village, Makati, Rizal; in SOUTH AFRICA by Multipet Pty. Ltd., P.O. Box 35347, Northway, 4065, South Africa. Published by T.F.H. Publications, Inc. Manufactured in the United States of America by T.F.H. Publications, Inc.

Introduction

One of the first animals that man was able to domesticate was the dog. In ancient history, cave men were so attached to their dog companions that they often were found buried with their pets. In more than one civilization, the life of the community was dependent upon the ability of dogs to hunt, protect, herd animals and pull heavy loads.

As our civilization progressed, more and more varieties of dogs have come to light. The long-legged, fast-running Afghan Hound from Afghanistan has been in use for 5,000 years by the nomads of the desert to run down gazelles. The Pekingese has been an old lap dog of the ancient Chinese, who for thousands of years considered it to be a holy animal and restricted their ownership to royalty alone. The Poodle has a long and glorious history as a companion, hunter and swimmer.

Terriers were used in Europe for killing rats, and spaniels were used for hundreds of years for hunting and flushing small animals and birds. Is it any wonder then that there are now over 150 million domesticated dogs in the world?

The sad-eyed appeal of this little Basset pup speaks volumes on the universal appeal of puppies in general. Photo by Isabelle Francais.

Breeds of Dogs

Your problem is either what kind of dog to select to suit your needs, or how to best handle the dog that you now have. In the U.S. the recognized breeds of dog are broken down into seven general groups: Sporting, Hound, Working, Terrier, Toy, Non-Sporting, and Herding.

The Sporting Group of dogs is that group whose primary purpose is to hunt game and large animals and to retrieve that game which is killed by their master. Among this group are the famous pointers, which have the ability to track down game and to freeze to a "point" when they have located the prey. Upon a command from their master, they close in on the game and assist in the kill. Retrievers, both Golden and Labrador, are dogs with great hunting and swimming abilities. They are dependable in sport and they also fetch and carry the game after it has been brought down by the hunter. Also in this group are the English and Irish Setters. They too are hunting dogs. Of the several kinds of spaniels (all of which are supposed to have originated in Spain, thus the name *spaniel*), the most popular is the Cocker Spaniel, both the American and the English. The English

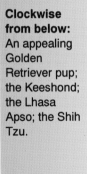

Springer Spaniel is a larger dog and is used primarily for field work. The Vizsla, a Hungarian dog, is often claimed to be the best all-around gun dog, but don't ever mention this in front of Weimaraner enthusiasts, for their claim

outstanding members: Afghan Hounds, Basenjis, Basset Hounds, Beagles (the most popular in the group), Bloodhounds, Borzois, Dachshunds,

is that the Weimaraner breed is the best hunting dog of all. So far, no *one* breed has everything. It is all up to the individual's taste in colors, sizes and abilities.

In the Hound Group, that group of dogs that is supposed to have the keenest scent, tracking

ability and the patience to follow and track for hours at a time, are the following

Norwegian Elkhounds, Rhodesian Ridgebacks and Scottish Deerhounds. The less popular members of the group are: Black and Tan Coonhounds, Foxhounds (American and English), Greyhounds, Harriers, Ibizan Hounds,

Otterhounds, Salukis, Whippets and Irish Wolfhounds. The Irish Wolfhound is one of the largest known breeds of dog.

In the Working Group are those dogs whose greatest abilities include guarding, drafting, and water-working. Included in this group

are: Akitas, Kuvaszok, Boxers, Bullmastiffs, Alaskan Malamutes, Portuguese Water Dogs, Great Danes, Great Pyrenees, Mastiffs,

Newfoundlands, Bernese Mountain Dogs, Rottweilers, St. Bernards, Standard Schnauzers, Samoyeds, Siberian Huskies, Komondors and Doberman Pinschers.

In the Terrier Group we find such as Airedales, Australians, Bedlingtons, Borders, Bulls, Cairns,

Dandie Dinmonts, Fox Terriers (Smooth and Wire), Irish Terriers, Kerry Blues, Lakelands, Manchesters, Miniature Schnauzers, Norfolks, Norwiches, Scottish Terriers, Sealyhams, Skyes, Soft Coated Wheatens, Staffordshires, Welshes and West Highland Whites.

The Toy Group, containing most of the lap dogs, are very well

known. They include Affenpinschers, Brussels Griffons, English Toy Spaniels, Italian Greyhounds, Japanese Chins, Maltese, Cavalier King Charles Spaniels, Chinese

Pomeranians, Pugs, Shih Tzu, Silky Terriers, Toy Manchester Terriers, Toy Poodles and Yorkshire Terriers.

Cresteds, Chihuahuas, Miniature Pinschers, Papillons, Pekingese, Miniature Pinschers,

members of this group include Border Collies, Belgian Sheepdogs, Bouviers des Flandres, Old English Sheepdogs, German Shepherd Dogs, Pulik, Shetland Sheepdogs, Australian Cattle Dogs, Corgis (Welsh and Pembroke), and Collies.

Top to bottom: Cardigan Welsh Corgi; Collie; Old English Sheepdog.

In the Non-Sporting Group, known as the Utility Group in Great Britain, you will find Boston Terriers, Bulldogs, Chow Chows, Dalmatians, French Bulldogs, Keeshonds, Lhasa Apsos, Poodles (Miniature and Standard), Schipperkes and Tibetan Terriers.

In the Herding Group are those canines who maneuver the world's bovine and ovine masses with remarkable skill and agility. Distinguished

SELECTION

A father was once faced with the task of selecting a puppy for his six-year-old son. Rather than risk buying a dog that the youngster wouldn't like, he allowed the lad to pick out his own pet. After studying the group of 10 puppies for an hour, the little boy finally exclaimed with joy, "Daddy, Daddy, get me that one!" pointing to a small puppy. "Which one?" asked his father. "That one, Daddy," he said, pointing to the tail-wagging puppy. *"I want the one with the happy ending!"*

Unfortunately, it may not be that easy for you to decide upon the puppy that you want. There are many things to consider. But first things first. *You should not buy a puppy on a whim.* You must be sure that your family members all agree that they desire a canine member of the family. You must remember that whatever kind of dog you select, be it an expensive rare purebred pooch or a mutt, no two of which look alike, it will require food, care, training, grooming and attention. It can be just as expensive to maintain a mutt as it is to keep a purebred dog.

If possible, buy a puppy between the ages of three and six months. It is advantageous to choose a puppy for three important reasons: (1) The puppy is not attached to anyone when you get him. (2) He is more easily trained. (3) You will have him with you longer.

When you select your breed of dog, keep in mind the following facts: (1) Small dogs are well suited to small apartments. (2) Large dogs are more expensive to feed than small dogs. (3) Do not keep large breeds unless they can have an area large enough for them to get plenty of exercise. Dogs allowed loose are a menace and can be taken away from you by law if you do not maintain them properly.

As far as the external symptoms of an unhealthy pup are concerned, look for these: (1) Runny eyes. (2) Cough. (3) Diarrhea. (4) Body temperature should be 102°F. if dog is normal. (5) Listlessness. (6) Red blotches on skin could be mange, ringworm, eczema or fungus. (7) Crooked legs can mean rickets.

When you buy your dog have an understanding that you will take your dog immediately to a veterinarian and,

if he advises you that the dog is in poor condition, that you will have the right to return the dog (usually you will be required to have a note from the vet substantiating your claims).

The question of which sex is better, male or female, is a matter

The Akita is one of those lesser-known breeds that has gained considerably in popularity over the past 10 years. Photo by Isabelle Francais.

of personal choice. Both can be lovable and affectionate.

If you plan to eventually breed your dog, naturally you will select a female. However, if you intend to keep her solely as a pet and do not want the responsibility of caring for a litter of puppies, then your female dog should be spayed. This surgical procedure on the female's reproductive organs renders her incapable of conceiving. Likewise, if you purchase a male dog as a pet rather than as a (potential)

stud dog, he should be neutered. Neutering will reduce a male dog's sexual tensions, and he may be less likely to roam.

Most every female dog has an estrus, or heat, period that occurs every six months or so. These periods last about three weeks, during which time a slight discharge is noticed. It is during this time that she must be mated, and the proper time is usually about the

tenth day after the start of flow. Naturally the female must be closely watched during these times, for she will not discriminate between male dogs when one is allowed near her. If it is your intention to breed her, you must select a suitable male. A purebred dog should be mated with another purebred dog of the same breed. Then pedigree papers and registration papers make the puppies that much more valuable. If you have a mixed-breed dog, of course you should have the animal neutered as there is *never* any reason to mate two

mongrels. Not only is over-population a devastating problem, but there is no way of knowing what kind of monsters you'll create. It is the continuous breeding of pure lines that guarantees that if you mate two pure breeds you will get the same type as the parents.

CARING FOR THE PUPPY

Don't forget that children always love small dogs, but when it comes to cleaning up after them or walking them for their relief and exercise, that may be a different story. Mother should be consulted

All dogs, whether purebred like these Japanese Chins or simply your everyday mongrel, require the same general care and maintenance. Photo by Isabelle Francais.

here, for more often than not, the dog will be more her responsibility than anyone else's.

It is assumed that you have a place in mind to keep the dog. Either the dog will be kept in the house or outside in a special doghouse. If you live in a cold climate, you wouldn't expect to keep a Chihuahua outdoors, so your next step should be to get a book and read about the breeds that interest you. This is one bit of advice you surely must heed. The world is full of

It's hard to resist the bright-eyed innocence of a new puppy, but be sure that you're prepared for the responsibility of a long-term relationship! Photo by Robert Pearcy.

wonderful dogs and so many great books on these dogs are available for you to explore.

The term "pet quality" to a breeder of purebred dogs means a dog that is bred from very fine parents, but one or more physical characteristics would ruin his chances of ever becoming a champion. (For example, the coat color of a Poodle should be an even solid color at the skin. Thus a black and white Poodle, though just as "good" a pet as his solid color brother, can never be shown because this color is not acceptable. Thus the mismarked particolor dog is "worthless" to the professional breeder of Poodles, and he will sell the dog very reasonably.)

If you check with all the pet shops, kennels and breeders in your neighborhood, chances are that you will find just the dog you want, at just the price you want to pay.

As his name reveals, the Scottish Terrier is one of the terrier dogs that traces his origins to Scotland. The breed has long been adored as a pet and long admired as a showman. Photo by Isabelle Francais.

Bringing Your Puppy Home

When you bring your puppy home, whether mongrel or purebred, you will need the following items to maintain him properly: (1) A harness and lead. (2) Food and a diet to follow. (3) A dog bed. (4) A suitable set of feeding dishes. (5) Toys to teethe on and play with. (6) Comb and brush. (7) Suitable bathing accessories. (8) Vitamin and mineral supplement.

THE HARNESS AND LEAD

Every puppy should be as full of life and pep as he can possibly be. As a matter of fact, that is one of the tests of a healthy dog. Not only is it nearly impossible to walk a puppy out-of-doors without a suitable harness and lead but it is extremely dangerous.

Harnesses are usually made of leather. Young puppies love to chew and if they can find nothing better, they will chew on the harness. A good hour-long chew will ruin a single leather harness.

A harness is placed over the shoulders of a puppy. It is supposedly more humane than a collar that goes around a puppy's neck, but it is the experience of many dog lovers that a puppy is more easily trained with a collar than a harness.

A lead, or leash, is the piece of chain or leather that connects the puppy to you. It should be 4 to 6 feet long and durable. A light chain is very satisfactory and, depending upon the quality of the chain, can either be cheap or expensive. Since the lead can be used as long as it lasts, it is definitely advisable to

Left: All well-stocked pet shops carry a broad selection of leashes and harnesses. Avoid using a choke collar on any new puppy. Photos by Isabelle Francais.

Opposite top: A portable puppy "play-pen" is a wise investment while acclimating a new pet. Art by E. Michael Horn.
Opposite bottom: Puppies are gregarious creatures, loving companionship.

Right: Puppies grow at a tremendous rate and must be supported by proper nutrition. **Below:** Food and water dishes should be, above all, non-tippable! Photo by Isabelle Francais.

spend a few extra dollars and get a fine lead, one that will not break and will be comfortable for both yourself and the puppy.

FOOD FOR YOUR PUPPY

When you have bought your dog, the person you purchase him from should give you the diet he has been maintained on up to this time. Keep him on the same diet as long as recommended.

A puppy should be fed four times a day. In the morning give him some milk (not cold) with a little cereal or cooked egg added (plus some vitamins and minerals). About noon feed him his heavy meal of dog food, cooked meat, egg

biscuit or dry dog food mixed with milk, broth or water. About five in the afternoon give him a little more fine dog food. Before you retire, some kibbled dog biscuits or puppy chow should be offered.

Keep up this diet until the puppy is 3 or 4 months old, then gradually skip the late evening feeding. When the dog is 6 or 7 months old he can be given the heavy meal in the evening and some milk fortified with vitamins and minerals in the morning. If your puppy doesn't seem to be thriving on this diet, have your veterinarian check him over and give you a more specific diet.

All food offered to your puppy should be clean and fresh, neither too hot

nor too cold. Feed your puppy at the same time each day and remove whatever food he leaves behind. Don't allow the food to remain on the floor until he finally eats it. On the floor it gets dirty, dusty and stale, and you will soon have a sick puppy.

Once you have selected a brand of dog food, stick to it. Sometimes a change in diet will give a puppy loose bowels. The question is often asked: "Why is one dog biscuit so cheap and the other so expensive?" The answer is simple. Some dog food companies manufacture their biscuits as by-products from other sources. For example: some bakers when faced with a lot of stale bread sell it for grinding up and making dog biscuits. On the other hand, many dog food companies go out and buy top-grade wheat. They prepare their dog biscuits according to a strict formula so that every time you buy their brand you get the same recipe. The latter type of dog food is naturally more expensive, but is worth the difference because it will keep your dog healthier and happier.

Always look at the label and check the protein content of the dog food you buy. Your average dog requires between 22 – 28% of his dietary intake to be protein. Protein, composed of amino acids, provides the material for tissue maintenance, growth, and repair. The remaining 70 – 80% of the dog's intake should be predominated by complex carbohydrates and fats (the energy foodstuffs)—with carbs composing about 40 – 50%, and fats 15 – 25%. Indigestible foods (roughage) are also required for sound health. Puppies generally require more protein and fats than older dogs, and it's always best to discuss your dog's diet and nutrition with your vet.

VITAMIN AND MINERAL SUPPLEMENTS

Regardless of how well you feed your dog, it is almost a certainty that your pet will not receive a balanced diet. To prevent

Natural bones are potentially dangerous and should never be deliberately offered to any dog! Art by Ann Marie Freda.

Young pups are accustomed to sleeping with the warmth and softness of littermates. It is the responsibility of the new owner to provide a warm, safe bed of the puppy's own to foster that sense of security. Photo by Isabelle Francais.

any of the many dietary deficiency diseases to which dogs are susceptible, you may be advised by your veterinarian to add a vitamin and mineral additive to the dog's diet. These are relatively inexpensive additives that will give your dog an ample supply of the rare ingredients that may mean the difference between complete health and constant illness. This is especially true of breeding females that often suffer calcium deficiency after they are bred and while

they are suckling their young.

Ask your veterinarian to recommend the supplements that are best suited for your breed of dog. Requirements vary from one breed to another.

A PLACE FOR YOUR PUPPY TO SLEEP

Every dog likes to have a place that means *home*. To a dog there is nothing more sacred than his own little bed. If you really want to make him feel like royalty, give your puppy a bed he will appreciate, a nice dog bed made especially for that purpose, with sweet-smelling cedar shavings in his mattress to keep the odor and the fleas away.

When you buy your puppy a bed make sure that it will be large enough to bed him comfortably when he is full grown. Ask your pet supplier to recommend the size best suited for your dog.

Locate your dog's bed on the floor away from drafts. A dark corner is good enough. Many people like to put the bed behind a chair where no one will see and disturb their sleeping puppy. Placing the bed near food is not a good idea because then your "Royal Puppy Highness" will get

into the bad habit of taking his food into his bed to eat it. Feed him in a different room if possible.

If your puppy prefers to sleep with you instead of alone, you have no one but yourself to blame. The pup's first night in his new home is likely to be a memorable one for all. After spending many weeks of life with a bunch of cuddly fellow puppies and nice warm snuggly mother, he has been suddenly taken into a foreign environment, and on top of that now he has to sleep alone! However, you must be firm with him that first night. Let him howl and cry. If you have a noisy alarm clock and an old doll, place them into his bed with him and let him sleep with some company. The alarm clock

The dog's first few days in his new home are a time of considerable anxiety, and providing him with a good chew toy can help relieve some of those doggie tensions. Photo by Isabelle Francais.

will make a comforting ticking noise and the doll will be something to snuggle. If you break down and take him into bed with you, he will keep you awake most of the night anyway, kissing your face and your feet, and you will then have started something that will be harder to correct the longer it continues.

FEEDING DISHES

All dogs, regardless of their breed, should be fed daily in the

same set of dishes. Unless your breed is a special breed that requires specially shaped dishes to keep its ears out of the water and food, an ordinary dog dish will do. Since dogs eat by grasping the food with their teeth or lapping it up, they must eat from a dish that is securely moored to the floor, either by its own weight or by the friction legs of a food stand. If you do not have a fairly stationary dish, the dog will

Mastiff puppies enjoy time spent outdoors. Photo by Isabelle Francais.

either tip the dish in his eagerness to feed or will push the dish against the nearest wall, possibly getting the wall dirty.

Ordinarily a dog needs two dishes—one for water, which should be available at all times, and one for food, which should be

filled at meal times, removed and washed immediately after the dog has eaten.

When selecting your doggie dishes keep three things in mind: (1) A good dish will last the lifetime of the dog. Don't buy a cheap thin pottery dish. Get a heavy plastic, metal or crockery dish or dinner set. (2) Get a dish large enough to comfortably hold the meal which will be necessary to feed your dog when he has matured. (3) Get a dish that can easily be cleaned, for you'll have to clean it every day!

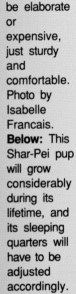

Left: A dog's bed need not be elaborate or expensive, just sturdy and comfortable. Photo by Isabelle Francais.
Below: This Shar-Pei pup will grow considerably during its lifetime, and its sleeping quarters will have to be adjusted accordingly.

TOYS FOR PLAY AND TEETHING

Puppies make interesting pets because they are playful, happy, loyal and

with resistance to chew on while their teeth and jaws are developing—for cutting the puppy teeth, to induce growth of the permanent teeth under the puppy teeth, to assist in getting rid of the puppy teeth at the proper time, to help the permanent teeth through the gums, to assure normal jaw development and to settle

lots of fun. But the owner of a puppy has certain responsibilities towards his puppy and one of them is to keep him occupied. Unless a puppy has proper teething toys, he will use your shoes, a corner of your best furniture or perhaps a piece of wood (like your favorite pipe). Biologically speaking, he simply must have something fairly hard to chew on to help him bring his teeth through his gums and to develop strong healthy teeth and gums.

YOUR DOG NEEDS TO CHEW

Puppies and young dogs need something

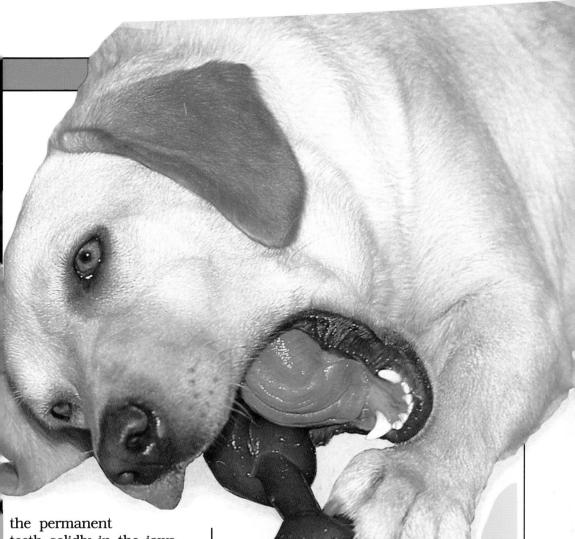

the permanent teeth solidly in the jaws.

The adult dog's desire to chew stems from the instinct for tooth cleaning effect, gum massage and jaw exercise—plus the need for an outlet for periodic doggie tensions. In the veterinarian's book *Canine Behavior* published by *Canine Practice Journal*, Dr. Victoria L. Voith writes:

"To reduce the dog's anxiety when left alone he should also be given a safety outlet such as a toy to play with and chew on. In fact, the dog may be encouraged to develop an oral attachment to this object by playing catch or tug of war with the toy at other times. Indestructible meat-flavored nylon bones are excellent."

Dental caries as it affects the teeth of humans is virtually unknown in dogs—but tartar accumulates on the teeth of dogs, particularly at the gum line, more rapidly than on the teeth of humans. These accumulations, if not removed, bring irritation,

This retriever wears a look of concentration as he gives his teeth a workout on a chocolate Nylabone. Photo by Vince Serbin.

Active chewing exercise can greatly reduce the accumulation of tartar and plaque. Art by John R. Quinn.

and then infection, which erodes the tooth enamel and ultimately destroys the teeth at the roots. Most chewing by adult dogs is an effort to do something about this problem for themselves.

Tooth and jaw development will normally continue until your dog is more than a year old—but sometimes much longer, depending upon the breed, chewing exercise, the rate at which calcium can be utilized and many other factors, known and unknown, that affect the development of individual dogs. Diseases, like distemper for example, may sometimes arrest development of the teeth and jaws, which may resume months, or even years, later.

This is why dogs, especially puppies and young dogs, will often destroy property worth hundreds of dollars when their chewing instinct is not diverted from their owner's possessions, particularly during the widely varying critical period for young dogs.

Saving your possessions from destruction, assuring proper development of teeth and jaws, providing for "interim" tooth cleaning and gum massage, and channeling doggie tensions into a non-destructive outlet

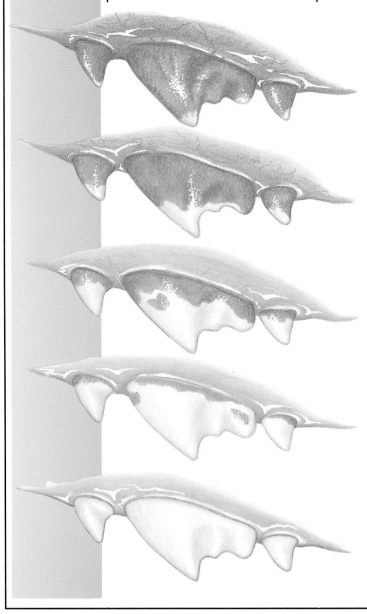

are, therefore, all dependent upon your dog's having something suitable for chewing readily available when his instinct

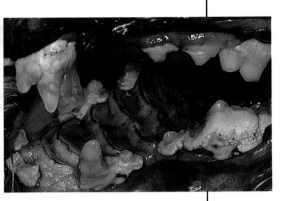

tells him to chew. If your purposes, and those of your dog, are to be accomplished, what you provide for chewing must be desirable from the doggie viewpoint, have the necessary functional qualities, and above all, be safe for your dog.

It is very important that dogs not be permitted to chew on anything they can break, or indigestible things from which they can bite sizable chunks. Sharp pieces, from such as a bone that can be broken by a dog, may pierce the intestine wall and kill. Indigestible things that can be bitten off in chunks, such as toys made of rubber compound or cheap

plastic, may cause an intestinal stoppage if not regurgitated—to bring painful death, unless expensive surgery is promptly performed.

Strong natural bones, such as 4- to 8- inch lengths of round shin bone from mature beef— either the kind you can get from your butcher or one of the variety available commercially in pet stores—may serve your dog's teething needs, if his mouth is large enough to handle them effectively.

You may be tempted to give your puppy a smaller bone and he may not be able to break it at that time—but puppies grow

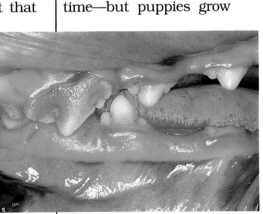

rapidly and the power of their jaws constantly increases until maturity. This means that a growing dog may break one of the

Left: This graphic photo shows a dog's teeth in an advanced state of decay.
Below: Providing safe and effective chew products can greatly reduce plaque and tartar build-up, and subsequent decay.

provides over the centuries only that which the animal needs to survive and procreate—and dogs have been domesticated for many thousands of years.

All hard natural bones are highly abrasive. If your dog is an avid chewer, natural bones may wear away his teeth prematurely; hence, they then should be taken away from your dog when the teething purposes have been served. The badly worn, and usually painful, teeth of many mature dogs can be traced to excessive chewing on natural bones.

Nylon bones, especially those with natural meat and bone fractions added,

smaller bones at any time, swallow the pieces and die painfully before you realize what is wrong.

Many people make the mistake of thinking of their dog's teeth in terms of the teeth of the wild carnivores or those of the dogs of

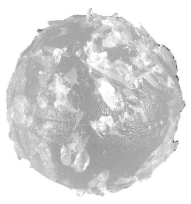

antiquity. The teeth of the wild carnivorous animals and the teeth found in the fossils of the dog-like creatures of antiquity have far thicker and stronger enamel than those of our contemporary dogs. Nature

are probably the most complete, safe and economical answer to the chewing need. Dogs cannot break them or bite off sizable chunks; hence, they are completely safe— and being longer lasting than other things offered for the purpose, they are economical.

Hard chewing raises little bristle-like projections on the surface of the nylon bones—to provide effective interim tooth cleaning and vigorous gum massage, much in the same way your toothbrush does it for you. The little projections are raked off and swallowed in the form of thin shavings—but the chemistry of the nylon is such that they break down in the stomach fluids and pass through without harmful effect.

The toughness of the nylon provides the strong chewing resistance needed for important jaw exercise and effective help for the

teething functions—but there is no tooth wear because nylon is non-abrasive. Being inert, nylon does not support the growth of micro-organisms—and it can be washed in soap and water, or it can

This dog obviously enjoys his Nylabone, but he should get his teeth checked by a vet at least once a year. Photo by Isabelle Francais.

be sterilized by boiling or in an autoclave.

Whatever dog toy you buy, be sure it is high quality. Pet shops, as a rule, carry the better-quality toys, while supermarkets seem to be concerned only with price.

Of course there may be exceptions, but you are best advised to ask your local pet shop operator—or even your veterinarian—what toys are suitable for your dog.

Nothing, however, substitutes for periodic professional attention to your dog's teeth and gums, not any more than your toothbrush can do that for you. Have your dog's teeth cleaned by your veterinarian at least once a year, twice a year is better—and he will be healthier, happier and far more pleasant to live with.

COMB AND BRUSH

Various breeds of dog have completely different grooming requirements. Some dogs need constant combing and brushing to keep their coats in good repair and acceptable appearance. Wirehaired breeds need combing and brushing for everyday care and their grooming might require stripping equipment as well. Shorthaired breeds might only require brushing, and a comb would be of little value. When you buy your dog, inquire about what essential grooming tools are necessary—and make sure you use them!

Not only should a brush and comb be minimum requirements, but a proper dog-nail clipper is also essential, for dogs that are not allowed outdoors sufficiently grow long nails that must be trimmed

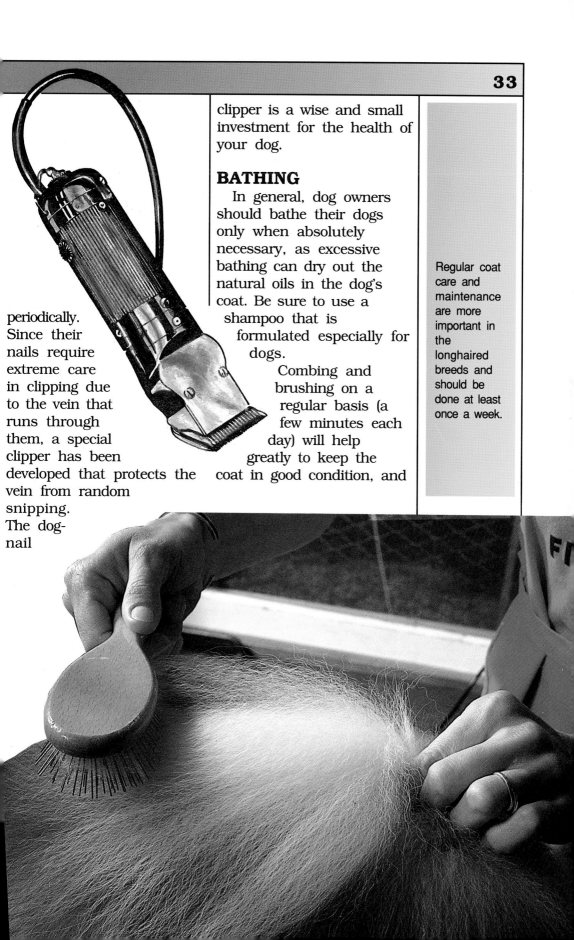

clipper is a wise and small investment for the health of your dog.

BATHING

In general, dog owners should bathe their dogs only when absolutely necessary, as excessive bathing can dry out the natural oils in the dog's coat. Be sure to use a shampoo that is formulated especially for dogs.

Combing and brushing on a regular basis (a few minutes each day) will help greatly to keep the coat in good condition, and

periodically. Since their nails require extreme care in clipping due to the vein that runs through them, a special clipper has been developed that protects the vein from random snipping. The dog-nail

Regular coat care and maintenance are more important in the longhaired breeds and should be done at least once a week.

if the dog owner practices these essentials, there is little doubt that his pet can get along with three or four bathings a year. Most dog owners are sufficiently disciplined to care for their dogs properly in this manner.

When bathing your dog you need only a suitable dog shampoo, a heavy towel, a large tub and a

has been thoroughly wet, add the shampoo or dog soap and work up a good lather. Then rinse him off the same way that you wet him down, being very careful that all of the soap has been taken from his coat. Be sure during the process that no soap gets into his mouth or eyes. His ears can be protected by stuffing them with cotton

If this large dog didn't enjoy being bathed, his owner would be hard-pressed to keep him in the tub! Dogs should not be bathed too frequently. Photo by Sally Anne Thompson.

strong back. The dog's bath is simple. Wet the dog thoroughly, using a plastic water glass to saturate his coat by pouring water over him while he stands in a few inches of warm water. It is assumed that you can bathe him in the bathtub or a large basin. After he

wadding.

After he has been thoroughly cleaned with two soapings and a thorough rinsing, you can lift him carefully from the bath while at the same time wrapping him in a towel. The dog's first reaction will be to shake the excess water from his coat with a violent shake. Unless he is covered with a towel and has had most of the excess water rubbed from his coat, expect a shower bath yourself from the water that will be shaken free by his typical shaking action.

In the wintertime it is safer to use one of the dry shampoos that are manufactured especially for dogs. Follow the instructions carefully.

If you are unable to bathe and groom your own dog, your veterinarian, kennel owner or pet shop personnel will be able to tell you who will.

Where it comes to the grooming of purebred dogs destined for show competition, it's best to rely on professional dog groomers for the best result.

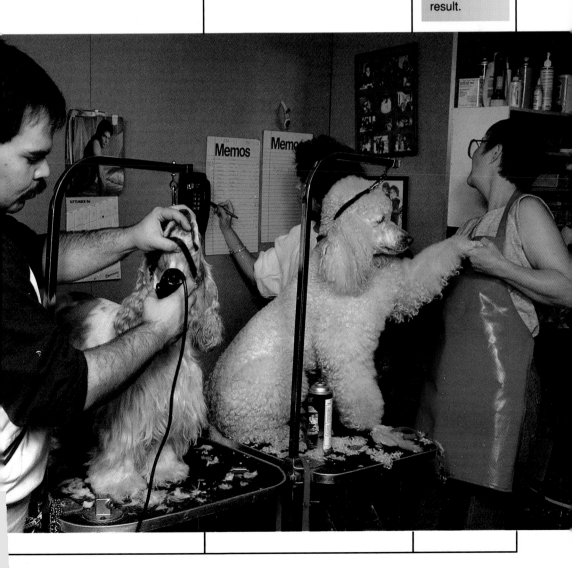

How to Train Your New Puppy

It has often been stated that the difference between an "animal" and a "pet" is *training.* The obvious truth of this simple statement makes it imperative that you consider training your dog from the minute you own him. The first training is to teach him to sleep quietly in his own bed and not to disturb your own sleep.

The second most essential training is his toilet training. For the small dog that will spend most of his time

When lifting your puppy, always support his hindquarters firmly and comfortably. Letting a pup dangle is both unkind and potentially dangerous. Photo by Vince Serbin.

indoors, toilet training is different from the larger dog that can be taken outside at any time. Small dogs, such as Chihuahuas, Pekingese and the like, can usually just as easily be trained to newspaper laid discreetly in the corner. This training is easily accomplished by using a housebreaking scent and putting the scent on some newspaper. The dog will be attracted to the scent and will get the general idea without much help from you.

Without a scent, or to supplement it, use some slightly soiled newspaper that has a bit of dog urine on it. Usually the dog will use that paper again and again. Once you replace it, the dog will have been accustomed to relieving himself on the paper. If you find him relieving himself in another location, then you must chastise him. Only do this when you catch him in the actual act. It doesn't take long to get the idea across.

For the outside dog, a dog that can be walked or let out into a fenced-in yard, the training is simpler. Immediately after every meal walk the dog until he relieves himself. As soon as he does his business, reward him with an affectionate pat. It won't

be too long before your dog understands what is expected of him and he will do it in a hurry.

For larger dogs that jump up to greet you every time you get home from shopping or work, the remedy is simple. When the dog jumps up grinning and

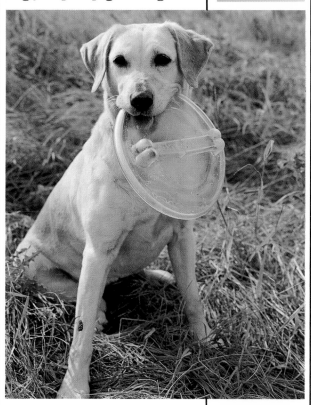

pawing, grab his front feet and retain your hold, meanwhile greeting him with good-humored tolerance. The dog finds himself in an uncomfortable position standing on his hind legs alone, a position not quite suitable or natural for one of the canine species. He

Most dogs take to playing with a flying disc naturally. Photo by Vince Serbin.

will soon tire of standing in such a way and begin to pull and tug to release his front paws on *terra firma*. Retain your hold in the face of this gradually more frantic struggle until he has become heartily sick of

The collapsible dog pen is ideal for confining your dog temporarily. Photo by Vince Serbin.

his position and the whole idea. It only takes a few days—and a few jumps—for this behavior to end.

If you have a dog that is a "barker" and you don't want him to bark (often people buy "barkers" to scare away thieves or intruders), merely reprimand him every time he starts barking. This will stop in time, but there are some dogs that can never be stopped from barking.

While walking your dog, be sure that there is an understanding between you and the dog as to who is the boss. Don't allow him to pull you in all directions. It is easy to train your dog to walk properly on the lead by holding the dog very close to your feet on a short leash. If he wants to pull, tug him back with a sharp "Heel!" It takes but a few long walks to have your dog walking closely beside you on a leash, and finally he will do the same on a loose lead.

The education of your dog is far from complete if he is merely housebroken and knows how to walk on a lead. If you want an animal that you can own with pride, you must train him in other fields. Training your dog intellectually distinguishes you from the next person, and your dog will only be as intelligent as you want him to be. Understand that your dog does not speak the same language that you do and that training is a long, repetitious process requiring a constant use of the same hand and word command. If you are to be a success with your dog, you must actually learn to think as your dog thinks. Dogs do things solely from their own point of view. There must be some reason for your dog to act the way he does. With this in mind you must place your dog in situations that are such that he cannot get out of them without doing as you desire. For example, if you want him to keep off the furniture, you must teach him to sit at your feet in the living room and to follow you wherever you go. When you allow him into the room, scold him severely when he jumps on the chairs; but when he sits at your feet, pet him gently and talk in a low, reassuring voice. It is not long before he learns what will reward him and what will result in punishment. This same treatment works for all social graces.

Remember: When you scold your dog, you must do so while the dog is in the actual act of disobedience. If you scold him later, he will not understand you and this will add greatly to his confusion.

Training your pup consists mostly of gentle firmness and repetition of commands. With careful training, any puppy will grow into a well-mannered, trustworthy pet.

How To Register Your Puppy

Owners of puppies are often mislead by sellers with such ruses from the term "registration papers." *Pedigree papers* are nothing more than a statement made by the owner of the dog and written on special pedigree blanks, which are readily

Purebred dogs, such as this Cavalier King Charles Spaniel puppy, are usually sold with registration papers. Photo by Isabelle Francais.

as leading the owner to believe his dog is something special. The term "pedigree papers" is quite different

dog also has a complete pedigree available as the usual run of things. These registration papers, which you receive when you buy the puppy, merely enable you to register your puppy, for usually the breeder has only registered the litter and it is the responsibility of the new owner to register and name the puppy. The papers should be filled out and sent to the appropriate address printed on the application, along with the nominal fee required for the registration. It is only this paper that is valid for registering your own litter if you breed from your puppy (be it male or female). Your signature is required on the litter registration as evidence that the dog has truly been bred with a purebred of the same breed.

available from any pet shop, with the name of several generations of the stock from which the new puppy comes. If your dog has had purebred champions in his background, then the "pedigree papers" are valuable as evidence of the good breeding behind your dog, but if the names on the pedigree papers are meaningless, then so is the paper itself.

Registration papers from a national dog registry organization such as the American Kennel Club or the Kennel Club of Great Britain attest to the fact that the mother and father of your puppy were purebred dogs of the breed represented by your puppy. Normally, every registered

Left: It takes a truly great puppy, a one-of-a-kind, to go best of breed in show competition. **Below:** Junior handling is an excellent way for child and dog to experience the dog show world. Photo by Sally Anne Thompson.

Keeping him healthy and happy is the responsibility of the owner. Ideally, the pet owner should establish a relationship with a trusted veterinarian.

What To Do If Your Puppy Becomes Ill

No book can teach you how to treat an illness of your dog. Not only is there the problem of treatment of the disorder, but there is a problem in properly diagnosing the illness. If your dog should become ill or manifest any of the signs or symptoms of a particular disease, do not waste any time. Contact your veterinarian immediately.

IMPORTANCE OF INOCULATIONS

To keep your dog protected as much as possible from major diseases, maintain a routine series of inoculations.

Distemper

Young dogs are most susceptible to distemper, although it may affect dogs of all ages. Signs of the disease are loss of appetite, depression, chills and fever, as well as a watery discharge from the eyes and nose.

Unless treated promptly, the disease goes into advanced stages with infections of the lungs, intestines and nervous system. Dogs that recover may be impaired with paralysis, convulsions, a twitch or some other defect, usually spastic in nature.

All new puppies should be inoculated against disease as early as possible. Annual boosters for distemper and rabies are advised.

Above: Cleanliness is indeed next to godliness when it comes to canine health. Are these pups looking for their "papers" so they can answer nature's call? **Right:** Administering medication by the lip-pocket method. Photo by Sally Anne Thompson.

Early inoculations in puppyhood should be followed by an annual booster to help protect against this disease.

Hepatitis

The initial symptoms of hepatitis are drowsiness, vomiting, loss of appetite, high temperature and great thirst. Often these symptoms are accompanied by swellings of the head, neck and abdomen. This disease strikes quickly, and death may occur in only a few hours. An annual booster shot is needed after the initial series of puppy shots.

Leptospirosis

Infection is begun by the dog's licking substances contaminated by the urine or feces of infected animals, and the disease is carried by bacteria that live in stagnant or slow-moving water. The symptoms are diarrhea and a yellowish-brownish discoloration of the jaws, teeth and tongue, caused by an inflammation of the kidneys. A veterinarian can administer the leptospirosis shot along with the distemper and hepatitis shots.

Rabies

This disease of the dog's central nervous system spreads by infectious saliva that is transmitted by the bite of an infected animal. Of the two main classes of symptoms, the first is "furious rabies," in which the dog shows a period of melancholy or depression, then irritation and finally paralysis. The first period can last from a few hours to several days, and during this time the dog is cross and will change his position often, lose his appetite, begin to lick, and bite or swallow foreign objects.

During this phase the dog is spasmodically wild and has impulses to run away. The dog acts fearless and bites everything in sight. If he is caged or confined, he will fight at the bars and possibly break his teeth or fracture his jaw. His bark becomes a peculiar howl.

In the final stage, the animal's lower jaw becomes paralyzed and hangs down. He then walks with a stagger, and saliva drips from his mouth.

About four to eight

Puppies are highly susceptible to many canine diseases before their complete battery of shots is administered. Photo by Isabelle Francais.

If done carefully, a dental check poses no threat to the dog-owner's fingers. Photo by Susan Miller.

be notified in the case of a rabid dog, for he is a danger to all who come near him. As with the other shots each year, an annual rabies inoculation is very important.

Parvovirus

This is a contagious disease that has spread in almost epidemic proportions throughout certain sections of the world. Canine parvovirus attacks the intestinal tract, white blood cells and the heart muscle. Overcoming parvovirus is difficult, for it is capable of existing in the environment for many months under varying conditions and temperatures, and it can be transmitted from place to place on the hair and feet of infected dogs, as well as on the clothes and shoes of people.

days after the onset of paralysis, the dog dies.

The second class of symptoms is referred to as "dumb rabies" and is characterized by the dog's walking in a bearlike manner with his head down. The lower jaw is paralyzed, and the dog is unable to bite. It appears as if he has a bone caught in his throat.

If a dog is bitten by a rabid animal, he probably can be saved if he is taken to a veterinarian in time for a series of injections. After the symptoms appear, however, no cure is possible. The local health department must

Vomiting and severe diarrhea, which will appear within five to seven days after the animal has been exposed to the virus, are the initial signs of this disease. At the onset of illness, the feces will be light gray or yellow-gray in color, and the urine might be blood-streaked. Death caused by this disease usually occurs within 48 to 72 hours following the appearance of the symptoms. Puppies are hardest hit, and death in puppies can be within two days of the onset of the illness. A series of shots administered by a veterinarian is the best preventive measure for canine parvovirus.

Parainfluenza

Parainfluenza, or infectious canine tracheobronchitis, is commonly known as "kennel cough." It is highly contagious, affects the upper respiratory system, and is spread through direct or indirect contact with already diseased dogs. It will readily infect dogs of all ages that have not been vaccinated or that were previously infected. While this condition is definitely one of the serious diseases in dogs, it is self-limiting, usually lasting only two to four weeks. The symptoms are high fever and intense, harsh coughing that brings up mucus. As long as your pet sees your

veterinarian immediately, the chances for his complete recovery are excellent.

INTERNAL PARASITES

Four common internal parasites that may infect a dog are: roundworms, hookworms, whipworms and tapeworms. The first three can be diagnosed by laboratory examination, and tapeworms can be determined by seeing segments in the stool or attached to the hair around your dog's tail. When a veterinarian determines what type of worm or worms are present, he then can advise the best treatment. A dog in good physical condition is less susceptible to worm infestation than a weak dog. Proper sanitation and a nutritious diet help in preventing worms. One of the best preventive measures is to have clean,

Above: A periodic check up may head off infections or irritations before they become entrenched and a real problem. Photo by R. Pearcy.

Fleas–important vectors of a number of diseases. There are many repellents and control agents on the market today. Art by Ann Marie Freda.

dry bedding for the dog, for this diminishes the possibility of reinfection due to flea or tick bites.

Heartworm infestation in dogs is passed by mosquitoes. Dogs with this disease tire easily, have difficulty in breathing and lose weight despite having a hearty appetite. The administration of preventive medicine is strongly advised. A veterinarian must first take a blood sample from the dog to test for the presence of the disease; if the dog is heartworm-free, pills or liquid medicine can be prescribed to protect against any infestation.

LYME DISEASE

Lyme disease is a bacterial infection that is transmitted to dogs by the bite of a tick infected with the spirochete *Borrelia burgdorferi*. The illness, characterized by a broad range of symptoms including chills, lethargy, fever, and pain and swelling in the joints, is most commonly transmitted by the deer tick *(Ioxodes dammini)*.

Your veterinarian can advise you about preventive measures for Lyme disease.

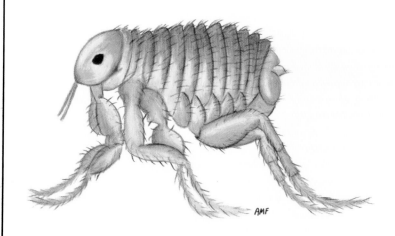

AMF

What Is First Aid?

By Dr. George D. Whitney, DVM

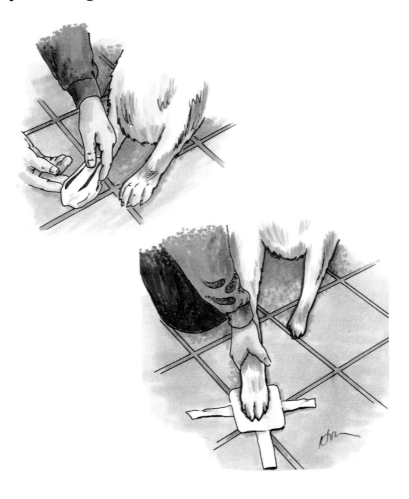

Paw pad injuries can be dangerous and should be cleaned and bandaged immediately. A vet should examine the problem as soon as possible. Art by E. Michael Horn.

This is an interesting question. It is answered quite differently by persons in diverse circumstances. To some, first aid is anything one has to do to make a dog more comfortable but for which professional services are not necessarily required. This definition includes treatment.

To others, first aid is whatever one has to do for a dog to save its life or relieve it of pain until professional services are available.

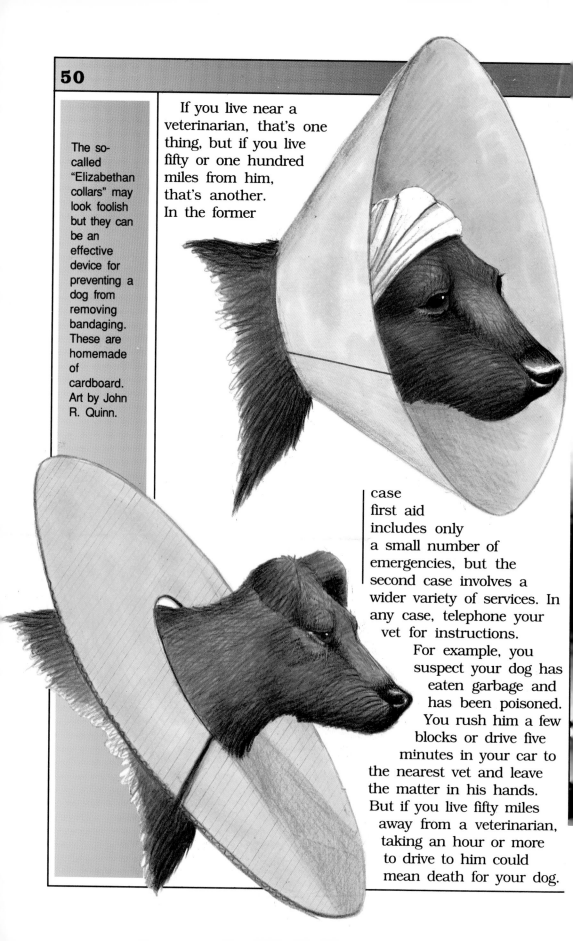

The so-called "Elizabethan collars" may look foolish but they can be an effective device for preventing a dog from removing bandaging. These are homemade of cardboard. Art by John R. Quinn.

If you live near a veterinarian, that's one thing, but if you live fifty or one hundred miles from him, that's another. In the former case first aid includes only a small number of emergencies, but the second case involves a wider variety of services. In any case, telephone your vet for instructions.

For example, you suspect your dog has eaten garbage and has been poisoned. You rush him a few blocks or drive five minutes in your car to the nearest vet and leave the matter in his hands. But if you live fifty miles away from a veterinarian, taking an hour or more to drive to him could mean death for your dog.

In one case first aid means rushing to a veterinarian, in the other treating the dog yourself.

In this section I will try to cover those first aid methods that may help you save your dog when there is no chance of immediately obtaining professional services or that will help you patch your dog up so that you can get him to the vet.

This is not a treatise that covers all of the ailments of dogs; it is simply a first aid guide.

PROTECT YOURSELF

In almost all first aid management the dog is in pain. He may also be in shock and not appear to be suffering—not until you move him, at any rate. Moving may cause pain so intense that he will snap at your hand. The gentlest dog should be expected to react in that manner. So, much as you love your dog, your first thought must be for yourself.

Tie his mouth closed so firmly that he cannot scratch the tie off. To do

No matter how friendly and trustworthy a dog may be, it should be muzzled if injured and in need of examination and treatment. Photo by Sally Anne Thompson.

this, tear up a piece of strong cloth four inches wide and three or four feet long, depending on the size of the dog. Make a loop in the middle of the strip and slip it over his nose with the knot under his chin and over the body part of the nose. Pull it tight and bring the ends back around his head behind the ears and tie it tightly, ending with a bow knot for quick, easy release.

Now you can handle the dog safely.

Should he attempt to get up and fight the mouth tie, you may have to tie his front legs together, and his back ones, or you could be severely scratched.

Occasionally a large dog goes berserk. How then can he be handled? You can try to restrain him by covering him with a large, heavy blanket. Now have an assistant apply the mouth tie described above.

Should you have to keep your dog lying on his side because of broken bones or other injuries, hold his head down with one hand

Your veterinarian can instruct you in the proper technique of administering medication orally. Photo by Sally Anne Thompson.

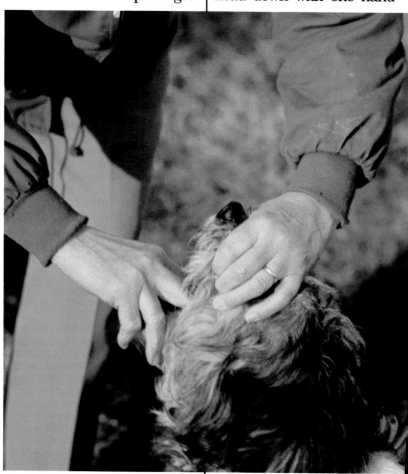

and with the other pull the hind legs out straight to the side; he can't get up unless he

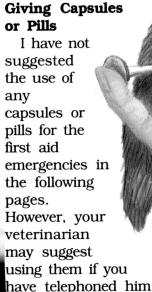

gets his legs under him.

HOW TO GIVE REMEDIES

To watch some dog owners giving pills, capsules or liquids to their pets, one would think it a great effort. It is not—when one goes about it forearmed with knowledge.

Giving Capsules or Pills

I have not suggested the use of any capsules or pills for the first aid emergencies in the following pages. However, your veterinarian may suggest using them if you have telephoned him for instructions, so here is the way they can be most easily given.

Presuming that you are right-handed, with your left hand place your palm over the dog's foreface and take hold of his lips, pressing them over the teeth with your thumb on one side and fingers on the other. He will open his mouth.

Twist your wrist so his head is turned upward.

With your right hand pick up the capsule or pill between your index and second fingers. Keep your thumb out

Gentle but firm restraint is the key to administering medications without mishap. Art by John R. Quinn.

of the way.

Quickly slide the capsule over the back of the slippery tongue and push downward as far as your fingers can reach. Let go and withdraw your fingers. Snap the jaws together and watch for

try to give capsules or pills holding them with thumb and index fingers. It is not possible in that way to push the capsule far enough back over the tongue for the dog to swallow it. So you

understand

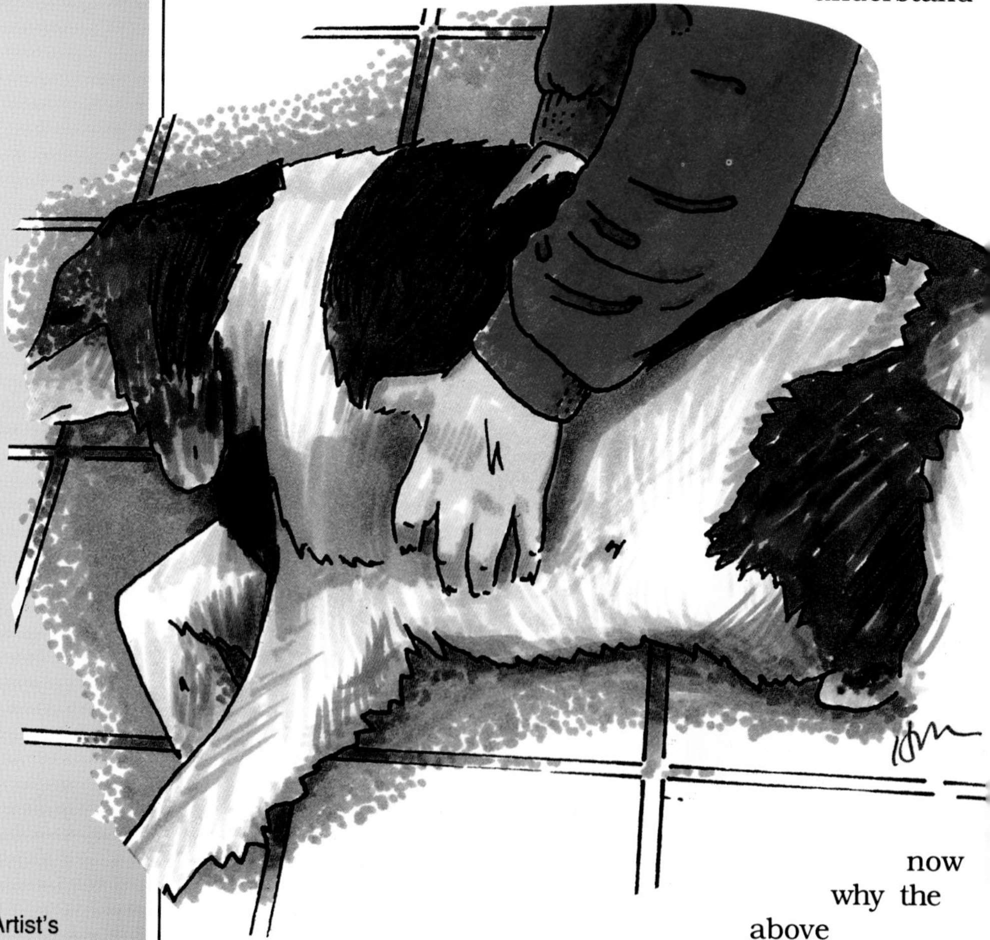

Artist's concept of carrying out chest compression on an unconscious dog. Art by E. Michael Horn.

a movement of the dog's tongue. You will see him swallow. Watch to determine that he makes no motion to chew or spit the capsule out. It sometimes helps to massage his throat.

Inexperienced persons

now
why the
above
instructions were given.

Administering Liquids

Have your dog sit. Insert the first two fingers of your left hand into the angle of the lips on the dog's right side. Some people find it more natural to use their thumb and index fingers. Spread the lips apart, pulling them slightly outward from the teeth, forming a pocket or funnel. Try not to elevate the head higher than a line drawn between chin and eye parallel to the ground.

Now, with the right hand tip the container holding the liquid and pour an ounce into the lip pocket, holding the dog's head slightly upward. The liquid will trickle past the tongue and he will swallow. Remain at the side, never in front of the dog, as he may cough and spray you with the liquid. When he has swallowed, give more and continue until he has taken it all.

In the case of peroxide, try to give the full dose all at once, because when it begins to fizz in the throat he may fight against taking more.

Should your dog be lying down and you are giving him liquids as a stimulant, try to roll him up enough so that swallowing will be natural; otherwise the liquid may enter his windpipe, with tragic results.

SHOCK

A dog in any accident, especially one involving a blow to the head or one in which some vital organ is damaged or ribs broken, will generally, mercifully, go into shock. He is less conscious of pain, but his condition is frightening. His pulse and respirations are slow, and they

The dog in shock should be carefully stretched out in preparation for placement on a blanket-stretcher. Art by E. Michael Horn.

may be very shallow. He may feel cold to the touch.

Don't try to apply a lot of heat. The best treatment is to cover him with blankets and let his own body heat build up. He

several thicknesses, drop it over his back and manage him by holding him within it.

If the dog is small and in shock, it is better to pick

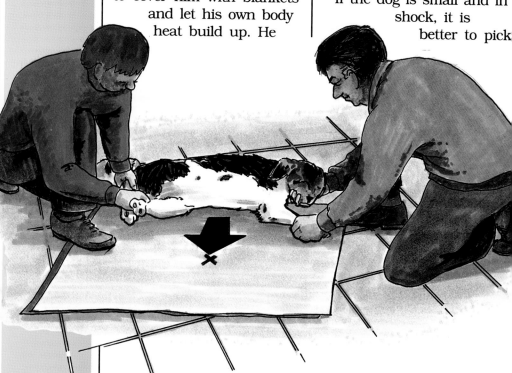

Sliding the injured dog onto the stretcher, care should be taken to avoid twising or bending the animal. Art by E. Michael Horn.

will then recover slowly and naturally. While he is in shock you may be able to get him to a veterinarian who will sedate him when the state of shock disappears and the dog becomes more conscious of his pains. A veterinarian has equipment to help him relieve shock. He may give oxygen or even use an artificial respirator. So if possible hurry the dog to him.

To handle a small dog you can fold a blanket into

him up by holding one hand under the front, the other under the hindquarters. This will keep him stretched out.

It is always better to roll an injured dog than to try to lift him. Suppose you find him lying beside the road after a car accident. Apply a mouth tie. Send someone for a blanket. Spread the blanket out and roll him over gently on it. Two people, one on each side, can make a stretcher out of the blanket and move the dog easily.

If no blanket is available and the injured dog must be moved, try to keep him as flat as possible. So many dogs' backs are broken in car accidents that one must think first of that possibility. Once he is out of harm's way, if he can move his hind legs or tail, his spine is probably not broken.

unguents, for canine maladies. Some simple home remedies can be used as first aid accessories. Here are some that can be found in most households, together with doses and how to administer them. The doses given are for medium-size dogs. Give more or less according to the size of your dog.

When lifting the injured dog, try to avoid an acute curvature of his body. Art by E. Michael Horn.

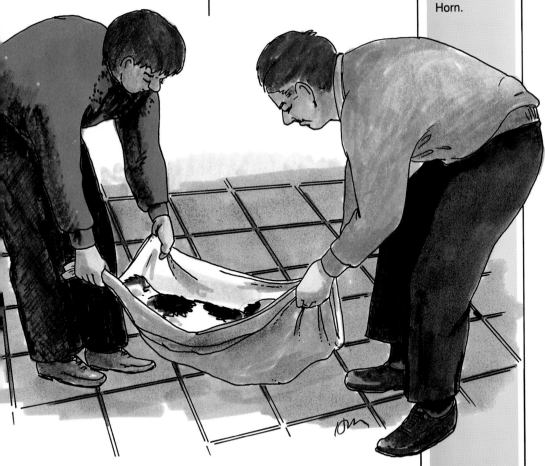

FIRST AID REMEDIES

Your pet shop stocks various medicaments, as well as lotions and

3% Hydrogen Peroxide

Useful in cleaning wounds. When applied to contaminated areas it produces a fizzing that stops when the peroxide loses its strength. This drug is an effective emetic. The ordinary drugstore strength mixed with an equal amount of water and given by the lip pocket method, so a dog has to swallow it, will cause him to vomit in about two minutes. If he does not, repeat in five minutes. Dose: 2 ounces of the mixture (50/50 water and peroxide).

Epsom Salts

This is a good physic and also an antidote for arsenic poisoning. Dose: 1 teaspoonful of Epsom salts in 2 ounces of water given via the lip pocket method.

Table Salt

An antidote for thallium poisoning. Also a fair emetic in an emergency. Dose: 1 heaping teaspoonful in one-third glass of water given via the lip pocket method.

Bicarbonate of Soda

This is to be used in acid poisoning and is given by mouth. For acid burns on the body or feet it is applied in a strong solution. Dose (by mouth): a rounded teaspoonful in 2 ounces of water.

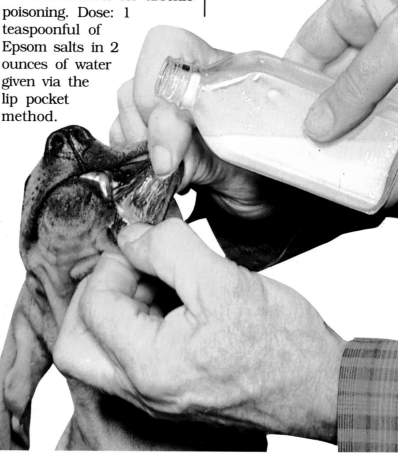

The "lip-pocket" method of medicating with liquids. Photo by Sally Anne Thompson.

Vinegar or Lemon Juice

The acid content can be effective to neutralize caustics or alkalis. Dose: 2 ounces.

Egg White

Antidote for mercury poison. Dose: the whites of six eggs after inducing vomiting.

Coffee

A remarkable heart and kidney stimulant. It is quite long lasting. Dose: 1 heaping teaspoonful of instant coffee in a half cup of water.

Karo Syrup (Glucose)

Give this to save dogs that have eaten certain poisonous plant leaves. Dose: 2 tablespoonfuls mixed with 3 ounces of water.

The position for heart massage on the unconscious canine. Art by E. Michael Horn.

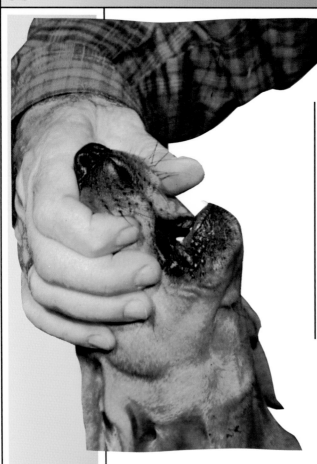

Gently squeezing a dog's muzzle will induce him to "open up." As always, gentle but firm is the watchword. Photo by Sally Anne Thompson.

Repeat many times. Stop as soon as you see or feel him breathing normally. This procedure has saved many a dog.

ELECTRIC SHOCKS

An electrical wire on the floor offers a temptation to any dog and especially to puppies. If a dog or pup chews a live wire, his mouth is usually burned, sometimes severely. He generally urinates and if he is standing close enough to a floor radiator or to a hot water or steam radiator which the urine touches, he may well be electrocuted. This doesn't mean he will die, but you can enhance his chances of living by quick first aid.

Keep away from the urine and shut off the switch that feeds the wire he has chewed. If you rush to his aid you too can be severely shocked. If you can't shut off the current, as for example when the wire is attached to a wall plug, then get a wooden cane or any dry wooden object—a broom, for example—and remove the wire from the dog's mouth.

Watch him to see if he is breathing. If not, feel his heart to determine whether it is still beating. If it is, give artificial respiration.

Mineral Oil

This is to be used to relieve constipation. Dose by mouth: 2 teaspoonfuls.

ARTIFICIAL RESPIRATION

After an accident, a dog is sometimes unable to breathe. Should yours be in this condition, first grasp his tongue; if he is unconscious, wipe out his throat with cotton or your handkerchief. Feel for a heartbeat and if there is one try gently pressing on the rib cage and quickly releasing the pressure.

What is First Aid?

Even if you cannot feel a heartbeat try to revive him. Press down on the rib cage and suddenly release the pressure. Repeat at ten second intervals. Stop occasionally to see whether he is breathing naturally. When natural respiration starts, discontinue your treatment.

He will be in shock. Treat him accordingly. If the tongue and lips are burned, take him to his vet. Sometimes burns that would disfigure him for life can be treated and sutured effectively, especially burns on the lips.

There are other ways in which dogs can be electrocuted. They may chew Christmas tree ornaments with electric connections or be struck by lightning, but shock is usually the result.

Above: Pills should be inserted as far down as possible. Photo by Sally Anne Thompson. **Below:** Cocker Spaniel pups.

The most effective and logical way of administering first aid for heat stroke: place the pet in a bathtub and bathe in cool water. Photo by Sally Anne Thompson.

DROWNING

This is an unusual occurrence, but first aid is usually needed for the unexpected. Dogs occasionally do fall into swimming pools or are pushed off bridges by mischievous children. The impact against the water has been known to cause unconsciousness, or possibly the head has struck against a submerged object, and the dog may drown. Dogs apparently drowned do not always need to die if you will render artificial respiration.

The first thing you must do is grasp out the dog's tongue and shake his head in a lowered position to drain the excess water out. In all of this, the speed with which you work is very important.

HEAT STROKE

Remember that the only appreciable way a dog has of reducing his temperature is by evaporating water from his throat and tongue. When water evaporates it becomes very cold at the point of evaporation. To reduce a helpless dog's temperature toward normal you must put this principle to work.

Suppose that you find your dog panting and salivating and in a state of collapse. How should you give first aid? The quickest way is to put him in the

The most effective and logical way of administering first aid for heat stroke: place the pet in a bathtub and bathe in cool water. Photo by Sally Anne Thompson.

bathtub and run cool water over him. You may be away from home. No bathtub. No hose in the backyard with which to wet him. Now what? Get some cool water, pour it over him and fan him to cause the water to evaporate. A newspaper or a wide board can be used as a fan and this will work, provided you put sufficient energy behind it and keep wetting him.

But suppose you are driving when the heat stroke occurs—a very frequent occurrence. Now what? Stop and get some water, if only a pint or quart, and after putting your dog on the floor

He may look mopey, but this little guy is in perfect health. Preventive care is always the best course to follow with any pet. Photo by Isabelle Francais.

of the front seat, open the ventilator and let the air flow over him while you keep pouring enough water on his body to keep him

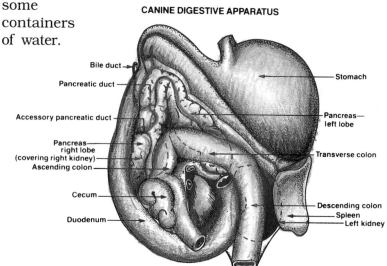

damp. This nearly always revives a dog. If you are travelling across a hot, arid area and your dog can't stand the heat, be sure to go prepared with some containers of water.

ventilate him.

Since dogs reduce their temperature via their throats, it was long believed that dogs with extra heavy coats were insulated against heat as well as against cold. While the outer coat does insulate against heat, it is better for his comfort to have him sheared all over except in the case of show dogs. The hair will grow in again and the chances of heat stroke are much less than when the heavy coat is left on all summer.

CANINE DIGESTIVE APPARATUS

Bile duct
Pancreatic duct
Accessory pancreatic duct
Pancreas—right lobe (covering right kidney)
Ascending colon
Cecum
Duodenum
Stomach
Pancreas—left lobe
Transverse colon
Descending colon
Spleen
Left kidney

Above: The canine heart is subject to pretty much the same ailments as the human organ with the important addition of heartworm.
Right: Diagrammatic view of the canine digestive system. Art by John R. Quinn.

Needless to say, any heat-struck dog should be moved out of the sun and out of dead air pockets to a place where the breeze can

HEART ATTACKS, CONVULSIONS

Old dogs often show typical symptoms of heart attacks. If your dog seems weak and prefers to lie down; if, when he stands, he tends to hold his legs farther apart than usual; if he pants, or after climbing only barely palpable. Likewise, by placing your ear on the left side of the dog's chest behind the elbow, you may hear the

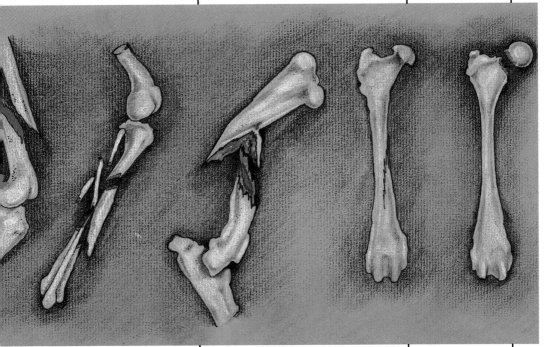

the stairs seems to have trouble in breathing, he may be suffering from a heart attack.

Put your index finger against the inside of a hind leg, as high up as possible; you will feel the femoral artery pulsing. In a heart attack this pulse may be heart beating feebly.

On the other hand, your veterinarian may find instead of a heart attack an inherited defect or heart worms, which live in the heart and which in large numbers produce

Above: Bone fractures and breaks can take many forms and are always serious.
Left: chubby, healthy retriever pups pose for the camera. Photo by Isabelle Francais.

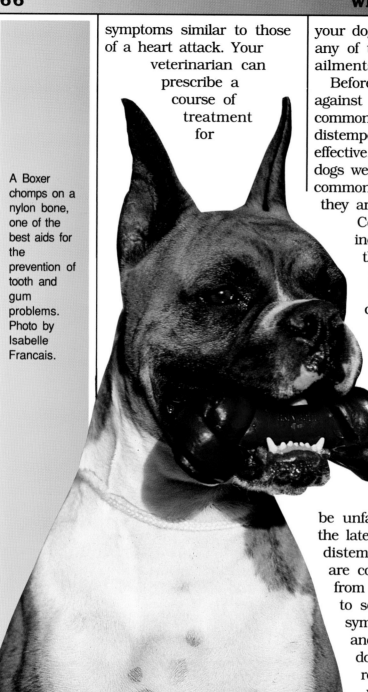

A Boxer chomps on a nylon bone, one of the best aids for the prevention of tooth and gum problems. Photo by Isabelle Francais.

symptoms similar to those of a heart attack. Your veterinarian can prescribe a course of treatment for your dog should it suffer any of the aforementioned ailments.

Before vaccinations against several once common diseases of the distemper complex were effective, convulsions in dogs were a much more common occurrence than they are today.

Convulsions can indicate epilepsy or they may, in puppies, be due to lumps of very coarse food in the stomach; but usually the convulsions indicate brain inflammation, often as a result of some viral disease. Very often the outcome will be unfavorable. During the later stages of canine distemper convulsions are common, ranging from localized twitching to seizures. These symptoms may abate and reappear. Many dogs die but some recover. As the dog recovers from an attack, the dog is usually dizzy. This is not rabies; a rabid dog does not recover.

Treatment: Do not

pick up a convulsive dog. Have faith that he will soon be over it. Clean him up and take him to the veterinarian, where you can leave him for diagnosis and treatment. He may be on a downhill course. He may recover naturally or he may be left with a twitch in some groups of muscles, depending upon what area in his brain is damaged.

Certainly you do not want him having repeated convulsions at home, so unless his veterinarian advises you that he is better off at home let him manage the pet's treatment.

Loose-skinned breeds, such as the Shar-Pei, require more attention to skin and coat care than most other dogs. Photo by Isabelle Francais.

Above: Good nutrition, the key to robust canine health. **Right and below:** Your puppy should be supervised when he's exploring field or garden.

CUTS AND WOUNDS

First aid in these accidents consists of stopping the bleeding, cleaning the wound and preventing infection. A small amount of bleeding is often desirable as it washes away some impurities. When skin is torn leaving a raw area and is left untreated for even twenty-four hours, it will shrink and be difficult to stretch back into place when the veterinarian attempts to cover the raw area by suturing the skin.

If you cannot quickly reach your veterinarian, try to clean out the wound. Gently swab out any dirt or grease, and flood the area with peroxide to help loosen the foreign matter. If there is a flap of skin which you can draw across the area, do so, and gently

bandage it in place, thus keeping the skin moist.

If the damaged area is not large, letting the dog lick it clean is one of the best possible treatments. He will remove the foreign matter, and the rough tongue surface will rid the wound of all dead tissue. When he is

finished, pull the skin flap over and bandage the area.

SPLINTERS

Dogs, like human beings, are frequently pierced by splinters, the difference being that with dogs splinters usually penetrate their feet. If you see a dog limping or running on three legs, especially if he chews at the lame foot,

examine the foot carefully. If you locate the splinter or other sharp object, tie his mouth and try to pull the object out with

tweezers. If it does not come out, call the veterinarian. Splinters left in the flesh too long can cause tetanus (lockjaw), especially if pus develops. The veterinarian will know whether the dog should be given antitoxin.

Not all splinters enter the feet. The dog will help you locate the offender by

These common weeds and garden plants could cause illness in puppies if chewed or eaten. **Clockwise from top:** Hemlock; Nightshade; Larkspur; and Lily-of-the-Valley. Art by John R. Quinn.

Puppies love to romp in wooded areas, but close supervision is called for as many dangers may lurk in extensive, rugged terrain. Photo courtesy Sara Chapman.

trying to pull it out himself.

ELASTIC BANDS

Mischievous children frequently put elastic bands around dogs' necks, ears, tails and legs, and the bands may go unsuspected until they have actually cut into or through the skin. Generally an obnoxious odor is the signal. The cut will ooze and attract flies. When elastic bands have been left on too long, ears and tails have actually suffered gangrene.

First aid consists of hooking out the elastic and cutting it, pulling it from its bed and trying to clean out the area. This is often a tedious job because hair may have been pressed into the cut by the band, and dirt may have accumulated. There is usually a great deal of suturing to be done, so let your veterinarian handle the work properly as soon as possible.

is impossible. You will recall having read in

POISONING

There are some basic facts you should understand about poisoning. There are many kinds of poisons. Some, like thallium, can act slowly or very quickly, depending on the amount ingested. Some, like cyanide, act so fast that saving a dog

detective stories whereby a person drinking a potion with cyanide in it dies before he has finished the contents of the glass.

When poisoning is suspected, try to determine what poison is involved. If you see your dog dig up a mole poison you have planted in a mole burrow, quickly find the

container from which you took the poison bait and read the composition. By knowing the poison you can supply the antidote and treatment. In almost all cases, the first thing to do is empty the dog's stomach.

Sometimes a neighbor has been using poison. Should your dog swallow some, hurry to the neighbor and get him to read the composition of the toxic drug and the antidote. It may be some poison that you will not find mentioned here. Read the antidote, which is always listed on the package.

Whole books dealing with poisons have been published. Obviously we can consider only the more common ones here. If you suspect that your dog has been poisoned, phone your veterinarian for instructions.

Raccoons and other "suburban" wild animals may tangle with an aggressive dog and, if infected, pass rabies to the pet. Photo by Dr. Herbert R. Axelrod.

Kennel cleanliness is an important factor where numbers of dogs are confined. Unsanitary conditions invite disease!

Some poisons are corrosive; they burn what they touch—mouth, throat, gullet, stomach. In such cases unless almost immediate antidotes are given, it is too late to help. Because the stomach contains fluid, the damage done by some acids and alkalis is not quite as immediate as the same corrosives would be if poured over the skin of your forearm, for example. The way to counteract their damage is to neutralize them by trying to keep the poisons from corroding deeper into tissue.

It is equally important to remember that once an area has been damaged, it requires a long time to heal. The dog may be unable to eat for weeks, yet still be alive when his organs have healed. Imagine a large area of your skin burned by a strong acid. How many weeks will it be before the area has healed and skin has grown slowly across to cover it? While the dog is recuperating from a poisoning case this fact must be taken into consideration. I assume that you will try to give first aid and then hustle your pet to the veterinarian. Don't expect

the caustic may be left over and be thrown into the garbage. It takes but a few crystals to cause damage. *Symptoms:* Intense salivation, often followed by nausea, vomiting and expression of pain. *Treatment:* Neutralize the caustic by giving vinegar or lemon juice.

He looks inquisitive, and he is! Keep all household solvents and chemicals well out of reach!

him to wave a wand and all the tissues will be healed. No, they will take time and you must be a patient nurse during the healing process.

The following common poisons are listed in the order of their prevalence in my own experience.

Alkalis

The most common one is drain cleaner. When cleaning drains some of

Food Poisoning

Partially decomposed food in which certain food poisoning organisms have developed can be deadly, but usually there is time to save the dog. *Symptoms:* Trembling is usually the first sign, followed by prostration. When botulism poisoning is the cause, the dog becomes limp all over as if he lacked strength in his muscles, especially the neck.

Frequently the dog is unable to vomit voluntarily. *Treatment:* Empty the stomach, using peroxide, and when the nausea has ended give Epsom salts or some other quick-acting laxative.

Cyanide

Many cyanide poisonings are malicious, but not all. Because so many suburbanites are troubled by ground moles, thousands of packages of mole poisons are sold annually. The property owner buries them in mole burrows and the cyanide in them kills the moles. Unfortunately, curious dogs see or smell the place where the ground has been freshly dug, scratch up the mole poison and eat it. Many mole poisons contain cyanide, but not enough to produce a fatal effect. *Symptoms:* If you think your dog has swallowed some, take a sniff of his breath and the odor of almond will be quite clear. Look at his gums and tongue, which will be blue. He will show pain and have trouble breathing. *Treatment:* Give peroxide (50-50 with water). You may save him. But let your veterinarian carry on from there.

Warfarin

This common rodent poison, fortunately for dog owners, must be eaten for three or four meals to actually cause death. Death is caused by internal bleeding. Even two meals will cause some ill effects. Symptoms: Paleness of the gums, lips and tongue. General overall weakness. *Treatment:* In the early stages, keeping the dog

In any case of suspected poisoning, get your dog to a veterinarian immediately! If possible, identify the poison source. Photo by Robert Pearcy.

away from warfarin will enable him to recover. In the last stages no treatment is known. Transfusions have been given, but they produce only temporary

circulating in the blood-stream damages internal organs. The quickest possible treatment is essential. Peroxide, which causes vomiting, is the antidote. Even though you

Among the many possible poisons threatening the dog, toad poisoning is a very real one. This ceramic replica, however, is assuredly a harmless playmate.

improvement. Consult your veterinarian.

Phosphorus
This is another rodent poison. Its effects on dogs are cruel. *Symptoms:* Often causes writhing pain. The breath always has a garlic odor; diarrhea begins quite rapidly. The dog first becomes prostrated, then goes into a coma and dies. *Treatment:* Phosphorus

save your dog's life it may be a long time before he acts like his old self.

Thallium
This is an insect and rodent poison. It is a slow poison, symptoms sometimes develop days after ingestion, at which time only supportive veterinary treatment is effective. *Symptoms:* When large amounts have been

ingested, salivating and drooling, nausea and vomiting, diarrhea and expressions of pain appear. *Treatment:* Table salt given as quickly as possible after ingestion of the poison.

base paint) complicates the problem. *Symptoms:* Tell-tale paint around the dog's face and lips or paint chips on the body should make one suspicious, especially when he exhibits pain in the abdomen, perhaps trembles, breathes rapidly and constantly moves about until he becomes prostrated.

Stuffed toys and other destructible items are not recommended for the active puppy. Bits and pieces may be torn off and swallowed. Art by John R. Quinn.

Paint

This covers a broad area. What actually poisons are the pigments used in its composition, and the lead in the white lead which was used to give paint substance and adhesive properties. Paris green was sometimes used as a pigment. This is an arsenical, and any dog that has eaten old green paint should be considered a possible poisoning suspect and be properly treated. The lead in the paint (if it is a lead-

Treatment: Empty the stomach, and after the nausea has subsided give a teaspoonful of Epsom salts in water. The lead part is the least dangerous, but the arsenic from the Paris green may, if much has been absorbed from the paint, mean a protracted period of convalescence.

Strychnine

Those who use strychnine to poison rodents or other varmints frequently poison dogs too. Like cyanide, strychnine poisoning can be malicious. *Symptoms:* The typical violent twitching and trembling between short periods of quiet can never be forgotten by anyone who has seen a dog with strychnine poisoning. These tremblings usually end in death. The duration of suffering depends on how much poison was consumed. *Treatment:* If you can take your dog to the vet alive, the chances are that he can save him. He will inject a drug that will counteract the trembling and empty the stomach, usually in that order.

When allowing young children to rough-and-tumble play with puppies, be sure to keep a supervisory eye on things! Photo by Vince Serbin.

Copper

Copper is occasionally eaten in the form of copper sulphate. Dogs have chewed corroded areas over copper pipes and been made sick, but the ingredients in spray materials most commonly cause poisoning. *Symptoms:* Expressions of pain, sometimes convulsions, twitching and, if enough time has elapsed, the dog may void blue-colored stools. *Treatment:* Use peroxide to induce vomiting, provided you can treat the pet soon after he has eaten the copper. Better, let your veterinarian treat him.

Plant Sprays

These consist of a wide variety of drugs, with new ones coming on the market every year. For some there are no antidotes. The old culprits were mostly arsenicals and copper.

Chlordane

Chlordane has been sprinkled on lawns or gardens to kill grubs or around the base of homes to eradicate termites, and is an ever present danger for all animals. It is a slower poison than some. If you can't get to a veterinarian quickly, induce vomiting immediately.

Sodium Fluoride

This is sprinkled on floors and the lower shelves of closets to destroy roaches and ants. Dogs often drop bones or meat on it, then eat the meat and are poisoned. Induce immediate vomiting; then get to the vet.

It's unfortunate, but even a lawn may be unsafe as a puppy playground if it has been treated with fungicides or insecticides. Photo by Isabelle Francais.

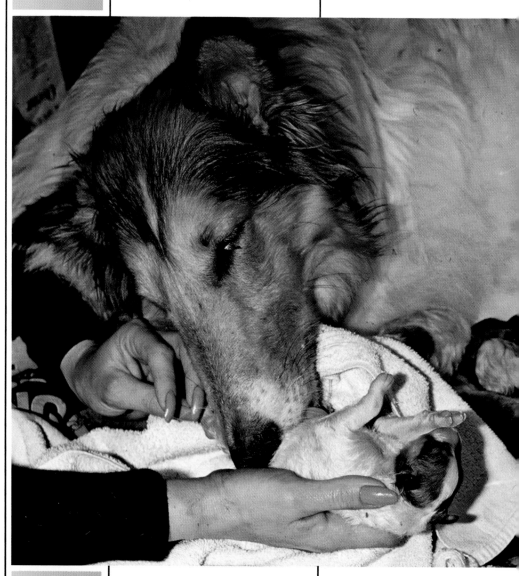

A whelping mother should not be disturbed unless a real problem arises during the birth process.

Ant and Roach Traps

For decades now, man has been developing and utilizing poisons to combat his ever-present ant and roach pests. In the past, thallium and arsenic were the chemicals of choice, but, fortunately, today "safe" poisons are being developed. Still, though, no matter how safe a product is stated as being, it must be suspected by the responsible dog owner, who is no different than the parent in this respect.

Radiator Antifreeze

This is often ethylene glycol. It may drip from a leak and, since it tastes sweet, dogs are tempted to lap it up. This substance changes to oxylic acid, which does the real poisoning. *Symptoms:* Chiefly pain and nausea. *Treatment:* If you are sure the dog has lapped antifreeze, empty his stomach and give a teaspoonful of bicarbonate of soda dissolved in water; then consult your vet.

Chocolate

The theobromine in black cooking chocolate, similar to caffeine in coffee, is very concentrated. Many dogs have stolen and eaten bars of this which, while it may not have killed them, have produced such symptoms of shaking that their actions were frightening. *Treatment:* Empty the stomach by using peroxide. Then let your veterinarian carry on. He may inject a sedative intravenously and quickly counteract the nervous symptoms. Be sure to tell him what medication you have given by mouth.

Laurel and Rhododendron Leaves

It is surprising how often dogs have been poisoned by these plants. No one has been able to discover the attraction. *Symptoms:* Nausea soon develops. There is profuse salivation and a general weakness. *Treatment:* Even if you know the dog has vomited, produce more with peroxide. Follow with Epsom salts for a physic.

This pooch may have exotic tastes in accessories, but exotic foods, such as rich chocolate, are a dietary no-no! Photo by Isabelle Francais.

Sleeping Pills

It may surprise you to know that many dogs somehow manage to find and eat sleeping pills. They must swallow them whole or the bitterness would cause the drug to be rejected. *Symptoms:* Should your dog come home and go into a deep sleep, suspect barbiturate poisoning. *Treatment:* Before he is too deeply unconscious to be able to swallow, empty his stomach with peroxide and give him half a cup of strong coffee. Then take him to the veterinarian.

BREEDING ACCIDENTS

A question sometimes asked of veterinarians is what to do when a pair of dogs is found sexually united, causing embarrassment. How to separate them? Policemen should know, but few do, and they are among those who telephone an expert for information.

All kinds of methods have been tried, from throwing water on them to the use of kind words.

Dogs remain united from fifteen to forty-five minutes. Think what would happen to a pair of breeding wolves if they could not separate quickly when danger approached! A fright will cause the dog's penis to shrink quickly, so frighten him— the bitch does not control the tying.

If you can find something to make a loud noise, use it.

The slamming of a board on the sidewalk will make a frightening sound. Or pound on a metal pan

These Husky twins present the picture of health hoped for in all dog owners.

with a heavy spoon or stick.

Accidental Breeding

Every year thousands of bitches are bred accidentally. While in heat almost any bitch will endeavor to escape, and males will perform unusual feats to get into their quarters to breed with them.

Accidental breeding presents a real problem to the owner, because abortion can be a dangerous (and expensive) alternative, due largely to the multiple fetuses involved in canine

pregnancies.

It is best that pet owners neuter their dogs and leave breeding to the professionals. This is the responsible approach in that it both reduces the animal's risk of cancer and prevents contribution to the severe overpopulation of dogs today.

The Birth of Puppies

The best solution is to be prepared. Give the bitch a place where she can whelp undisturbed. She will clean the puppies, licking off any fetal membranes that may cling to them. She will chew off the cord and eat the afterbirth, leaving her nest as clean as possible of all but fluids that escape.

Some people fill her whelping bed with old cloths. These frequently become mixed up with the puppies and the mother accidentally smothers them. If you live where you can buy soft straw or hay, make a bed for her in the shape of a large saucer. The pups will roll into a pile at the bottom of it.

If you live in the city, put several thicknesses of absorbent cloth on the floor of the whelping box and tack it down so it will remain flat. Change it after whelping is over.

Good nutrition and attention to prenatal care will result in healthy, bright-eyed pups like these Dobermans. Photo by Isabelle Francais.

Below and facing page: Guns and dogs do mix—if the dog has been carefully trained and the owner uses care and common sense when hunting with his dog.

Sometimes first aid is called for during whelping. If the mother is actively straining without producing a puppy, the youngster may be presented backward, a so-called "breech" birth. Careful assistance with a well-lubricated finger to feel for the puppy or to ease it back may help, but never attempt to pull it out by force. This could cause serious damage, so seek the services of an expert—your veterinarian or an experienced breeder.

HUNTING AND FISHING WOUNDS

Many a rabbit hunter has missed the rabbit and shot his dog. The dog will usually scream in pain and will frequently run for some distance. He may be difficult to find. When he has been found he may be in shock, the severity of which depends on the number of pellets and the force behind them. He may even appear dead and will have to be revived by artificial respiration. Do not try to remove the pellets. That's a job for a veterinarian, who will X-ray him and take out all he can find, especially those in dangerous locations, such as joints, where they can cause lameness. Some of the pellets will be lodged against bones; others may be loose in muscles, where they can cause pain with every movement. If the veterinarian does not find them all on the first visit, further X-rays may bring them to light and they can then be removed. Sometimes a small cluster of pellets will be seen in one location. After removal of the mass, however, one may still remain.

Bullet wounds are another matter. Even a .22 caliber can snap a leg bone or even shatter it. This calls for application of a splint and a hurried trip to the animal hospital. Jaws, shoulder blades, and backs are often broken. This does not mean the dog must be destroyed, not by any means. The bullet may be extracted, fractures set and, if the spinal cord was not damaged or severed by the shot, the small chips of bone may be removed by the veterinarian. In time your dog may be as good as new.

Fish Hooks

A fisherman casting with a new rod may attach a lure that attracts his dog

and catch him instead of a fish! Or perhaps the dog snatches at an old worm left on a fish hook. Even lures with no bait have been bitten by dogs. Veterinarians will tell you that these are common occurrences.

Since most fishermen have cutting pliers as part of their equipment, it is strange how helpless they are at relieving their dogs of the pain caused by a fish hook through the lip.

It is only necessary to apply a mouth tie to the dog and cut the hook in the middle, taking half out from each side of the lip. If the hook is embedded in the lip, that is a job for the veterinarian, who will use a general or local anesthetic and push the point through the lip and then cut the hook into two pieces. Dogs have chewed lures with three sets of hooks, most of which have sunk into the tongue and lips. If your dog does that, don't try first aid unless a vet is not available. If you have to, cut the hooks to get the body of the lure out of his mouth, and when you can get him to the veterinarian let that expert remove the points of the hooks from their deep positions.

Puppies are all feet and nose and curiosity–the ideal combination for getting into trouble! Photo by Isabelle Francais.

Traps

Dogs occasionally come home dragging small animal traps attached tightly on their feet. Sometimes, however, they become trapped in a large animal trap and cannot free the trap to

drag it home.

Before attempting to remove a trap, remember the dog is usually in great pain. Therefore, protect yourself accordingly. Hold the dog's leg so the trap is on the ground. Put one foot on the spring on one side, the other foot on the other spring and press down. The tension on the jaws will relax and they will

open. Then gently pull the dog's leg upward and out of the trap.

Some smaller traps have a spring on only one side, making them easier to open.

Examine the dog's foot for trap damage. Sometimes small muskrat traps will not cut the skin though larger traps may sever skin and tendons. When that happens the repair is up to your veterinarian.

A small muskrat trap may not severely injure a large dog's foot but any larger traps may inflict tissue and bone damage. Photo by Isabelle Francais.

Porcupine Quills

If you live in areas where there are porcupines, don't take your dog into the woods from late afternoon on through the night without having a pair of pliers in your pocket. You may need the pliers to pull quills should your dog attack one of these spiny creatures. He may get a mouthful of long white quills, but usually his shoulder and forelegs are also covered with short black quills where the porcupine has slapped him with his heavy tail. This is his defense mechanism, and the tail quills are much harder to pull than are the larger ones from the back.

Here is a case of first aid par excellence. You may have no time to rush the dog to a veterinarian. If you have pliers, do the next best thing—pull quills. Later the veterinarian will anesthetize your dog who by then might well be in a state of shock.

Tie your dog to a tree with his leash so he can't run away. Put a stick in his mouth so you can examine the inside of the mouth, the tongue and throat. Try to pull every quill. Freeing the mouth of quills makes him feel better, and he will not frantically fight with his paws.

Next, remove quills from around the dog's eyes, over the joints and in the chest. Now pull all the quills from the rest of the body. If one breaks off, you

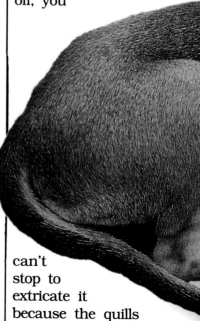

can't stop to extricate it because the quills

will be moving inward with every movement of the dog's muscles. Those which go inside the shoulder muscles will usually work upward, and during the next few days you will feel their sharp points protruding from the back just above the shoulders (the withers).

The quills in the front of the body will usually do little damage beyond causing temporary lameness until they have worked out, but those penetrating the area over the ribs, or the body behind the ribs, can cause death and should be the first to be pulled.

Examine the head carefully to assure yourself that no quills are pointing towards the eyes.

The next day and for several days after, feel your dog all over for points of quills and pull them out. You may wonder why the dog doesn't die of tetanus, but porcupine quills, as dirty as they are, rarely cause lockjaw.

What I have said may sound simpler than it really is. If your dog is a big one, heroic measures and all your strength and patience may be called for just to control him. Your leg wrapped about his body could help to restrain him.

BLOAT

Unless you own a Great Dane, St. Bernard, Newfoundland, or other large breed of dog you may never know the danger of bloat. But all giant breed owners have been told of the danger. Usually about five to six hours after a meal, gas develops in the stomach and causes the abdominal cavity to

Large breeds, such as the Great Dane, are particularly susceptible to the painful condition known as bloat. It can be fatal if untreated. Photo by Isabelle Francais.

swell to huge proportions. On tapping the side, it sounds hollow and drum-like. The ballooning continues until pressure on the lungs and heart becomes intense. In severe cases the dog may die unless the pressure is quickly relieved.

If you can hustle your dog to a vet in time, he will be able to help.

If it is too late, the dog, although relieved, may face a lingering death.

In the early stages it is sometimes possible to gently squeeze, prod and knead the abdomen, which may produce great volumes of gas to be expelled by belching.

For a stimulant, strong coffee may work wonders. A teaspoonful of instant coffee in a half cup of warm water, given to the dog by the lip pocket method, is enough for a fairly large one; two

teaspoonsful for a Great Dane or other giant dog. This is given after the gas has been let out of the stomach.

It is imperative for a vet to see such a case for many reasons, not the least of which is to determine whether the stomach has

bites occur too far from any help. Some vets advise making parallel incisions one-quarter inch deep through the fang marks in the hope that bleeding will

Venomous snakes, such as this prairie rattlesnake, have a vital place in nature but the bite of a large specimen can be fatal to a dog. Photo by Ron Everhart.

rotated out of position. If it has, surgery may be the only method of correction.

SNAKE BITES

There is very little one can do in the way of first aid for a dog bitten by a poisonous snake, unless the bite is on a foot or low down on the leg.

Treatment: Apply a tourniquet to try to keep the poison from spreading upwards. Release the tourniquet for 30 seconds every ten minutes and reapply. Hurry him to a veterinarian. Usually snake

partly wash out the venom. A sharp knife is necessary and, needless to say, the dog should be very securely tied, both to keep his mouth closed and to prevent him from running away. Suction to the lanced area could help.

Dogs used in the hunt, such as the German Shorthaired Pointer, are the most likely to encounter a skunk. Photo Isabelle Francais.

An alternative method of treatment is to pack the afflicted area with ice compresses and rush the dog to the veterinarian.

SKUNK SPRAYING

No one wants to keep a dog that has been sprayed by a skunk about his premises, waiting for the odor to disappear, though it will in time and more quickly in hot weather.

If your dog is sprayed, wash him with detergent and after rinsing, rub canned tomato juice into the coat, allowing it to soak in for ten minutes; then rebathe him with detergent and rinse. Repeat each step until the odor is gone. The amount of juice is determined by the dog's size and the thoroughness with which the skunk anointed the dog.

The dog may damage his eyes by rubbing them to rid himself of the odor and because the chemical irritates. However, it causes only a local irritation—never blindness.

FEAR OF THUNDERSTORMS

Many dogs actually suffer in thunderstorms. They let us know when one is approaching before we are conscious of it, thus allowing us time to give a sedative or tranquilizer previously obtained from the veterinarian.

Some dogs are less distressed when close to a loved one.

The cellar or an inside room may help such a sensitive pet, and playing the radio with loud volume often helps overshadow the thunder.

FREEZING AND FROSTBITE

Most problems of exposure arise after a dog has been injured, entangled in briers, or caught on a wire fence by his collar. Even if his body is stiff, if the heart is beating bring him into room temperature and raise his temperature slowly, depending on massage rather than artificial heating devices. This is one of the few times when whiskey may be of help as an initial stimulant. Later,

Above and below: Well-coated dogs like the St. Bernard and Samoyed are generally more tolerant of the cold—though less so of the heat—than other dogs. Photos by Isabelle Francais.

when the blood is flowing and pain may be present, it acts as a depressant. One tablespoonful with one tablespoonful of water and one tablespoonful of sugar should be given at thirty minute intervals for a thirty-pound dog.

True frostbite is slow to heal and your veterinarian should handle the problem. Antibiotics are often given after freezing and frostbite to prevent further complications such as pneumonia.

The warm-hearted Golden Retriever.

Some Simple First Aid Don'ts

Don't try to treat serious problems without a veterinarian's advice.

Don't heed the well-meant advice of the untrained, self-named expert.

Don't put hot compresses on a recent injury.

Don't put cold compresses on an old injury.

Don't leave a tourniquet in place for more than ten minutes without releasing it for thirty seconds.

Not really a basket-case–just enjoying his special hideaway! Photo by Isabelle Francais.

Don't put a bandage on an extremity too tightly unless the bandage is only temporary.

Don't overdose with home remedies such as aspirin.

Don't use human remedies on your dog without a veterinarian's advice.

Don't leave needles and pins and other lethal objects where a dog can reach them.

Don't permit your dog the luxury of running loose unattended; garbage, poisons and automobiles can maim or kill him.

Shar-Pei puppies. Photo by Isabelle Francais.

Don't leash a dog where he can jump over a barrier and hang himself.

Don't leave a dog in a motor vehicle in the sun with the windows closed; in the heat of summer don't leave him in the car at all.

Don't use whiskey for all your dog's ills—it's an initial stimulant, then a depressant.

Don't try to be your own veterinarian.

Black-and-white Cocker Spaniel. Photo by Isabelle Francais.

Index